www.claudiaespinal.com
Copyright® 2023 CR Espinal and Co
Todos los derechos reservados
ISBN: 979-8-9877227-0-1

Las Aventuras de Rodrigo

Escrito por Claudia Espinal - Ilustrado por Jayri Gómez

Para mis maravillosos hijos
Rodrigo y Mía Sofía.
Nunca dejen de soñar y
luchar por sus sueños.

Mamá

. . . .

A Yanir y Ricky.
Que su luz brille
para siempre.

Él es Rodrigo...

Y este es **Danny**,
su mejor amigo.

Rodrigo es un súper niño...
en busca de súper aventuras.

Pero cada vez que juega,
¡Hace una **súper travesura!**

Su deporte favorito
es la natación...

¡Le encanta asustar a su mamá
con un **súper chapuzón!**

Su capa mágica
en superhéroe lo convierte.

Quiere correr súper rápido
y crecer súper fuerte.

Un día en el parque,
Rodrigo tenía un plan...

Escalar para lanzarse
de un gigante tobogán.

Mientras subía, sus piernas
le empezaron a doler...

Tuvo que soltar a Danny
para agarrarse y no caer.

Rodrigo se sentía muy molesto, triste y cansado...

Pues no entendía por qué esto solo a él le había pasado.

Así que su mamá lo lleva
a un médico especial:

El Doctor Montero,
para ver qué estaba mal.

**Le pidió a Rodrigo
que lo escuchara bien**

**Porque tenía una condición muy rara
llamada Distrofia Muscular de Duchenne.**

La **Distrofia Muscular de Duchenne** hace que sus músculos vayan más forzados,

y al correr, nadar y escalar se sentiría muy cansado.

Rodrigo estaba triste
y sentía mucho dolor.

Pero su hermana mayor
le tenía un plan mejor...

Aunque la fuerza para
correr a veces se le va,

Rodrigo puede divertirse
hasta sentado en el sofá.

¡Hay un montón de cosas que **sí puede hacer!**

Como jugar videojuegos con su hermana junto a él.

Hay retos que debe enfrentar
para adaptarse a su condición...

Y convertirse en el superhéroe
de su imaginación.

En esta nueva etapa para Rodrigo, muchas cosas cambiarán...

Pero él sabe que su familia y sus amigos con él siempre estarán.

Dejar todo y empezar
de nuevo, le daba temor...

Pero su familia le recuerda
que lleva **un héroe en su interior.**

Aunque hayan días difíciles,
él tiene un súper poder:

Rodrigo siempre será valiente
para otros niños como él.

Claudia, Mía y Rodrigo son una familia de un país en el Caribe llamado República Dominicana. Cuando Rodrigo tenía 3 años, fue diagnosticado con Distrofia Muscular de Duchenne y sus vidas para siempre cambiaron. Al vivir en un país en vías de desarrollo fue muy difícil encontrar información, y más aun un diagnóstico.

Este tipo de diagnóstico es devastador para cualquier familia, pero ellos, juntos, decidieron luchar por la salud de Rodrigo, y trasladarse a New York, en los Estados Unidos, en busca de un tratamiento esperanzador para Duchenne.

Dejar atrás su país, su casa, sus seres queridos y sus vidas no fue fácil para esta familia. Enfrentar nuevos retos es difícil, pero a pesar de tener miedo, juntos siguen luchando por cumplir sus sueños.

Este libro nace con la intención de que más familias de habla hispana tengan recursos para educarse sobre la Distrofia Muscular de Duchenne, permitirles encontrar las palabras adecuadas para hablarle a sus hijos recién diagnosticados, a sus hermanitos, primitos y a sus amigos. Además, pretende seguir creando consciencia sobre esta rara enfermedad, y a la vez llevar esperanza a más hogares, motivándoles a luchar con todas sus fuerzas para juntos poder encontrar una cura.

Jayri Gómez es una ilustradora de libros infantiles de República Dominicana. Desde muy joven, Jayri supo que quería dedicarse al dibujo y encontró el trabajo de sus sueños ilustrando libros.

Como ilustradora, Jayri ha publicado numerosos trabajos con diversas marcas y editoriales. Como experta en multitareas, le gusta cantar o mirar videos mientras trabaja en su arte. A Jayri le encanta ver programas y películas de terror mientras trabaja. A pesar de su amor por el terror, su arte es tierno y colorido. Ella también canaliza estos colores en su vida diaria junto con la búsqueda de la paz interior y exterior. Jayri es una ávida fan de Harry Potter y Super Junior. Otros de sus hobbies incluyen comer y tomar siestas. Vive en Santo Domingo, con sus gatitos Momo, Ginny y Lilo.

GRACIAS

A nuestros ángeles en batas blancas:

Dra. María Emilia Yapor,
Dr. Juan Tapia, Dr. DeVivo
y Ameneh Masud.

A Samuel Vásquez.
Sin ti, este libro no existiera.

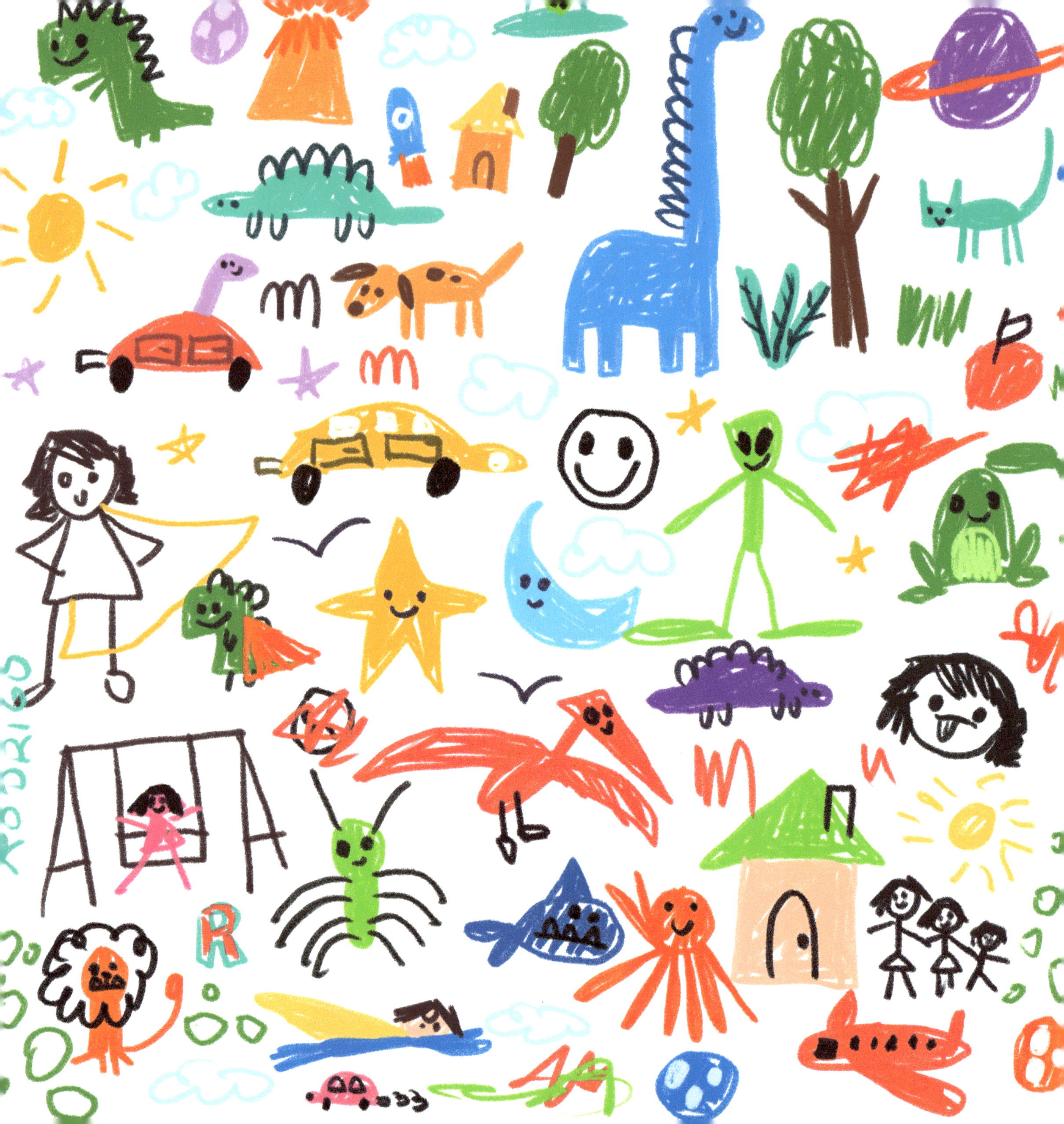
RODRIGO
R

RODRIGO Y DANY

SUPER RODRI

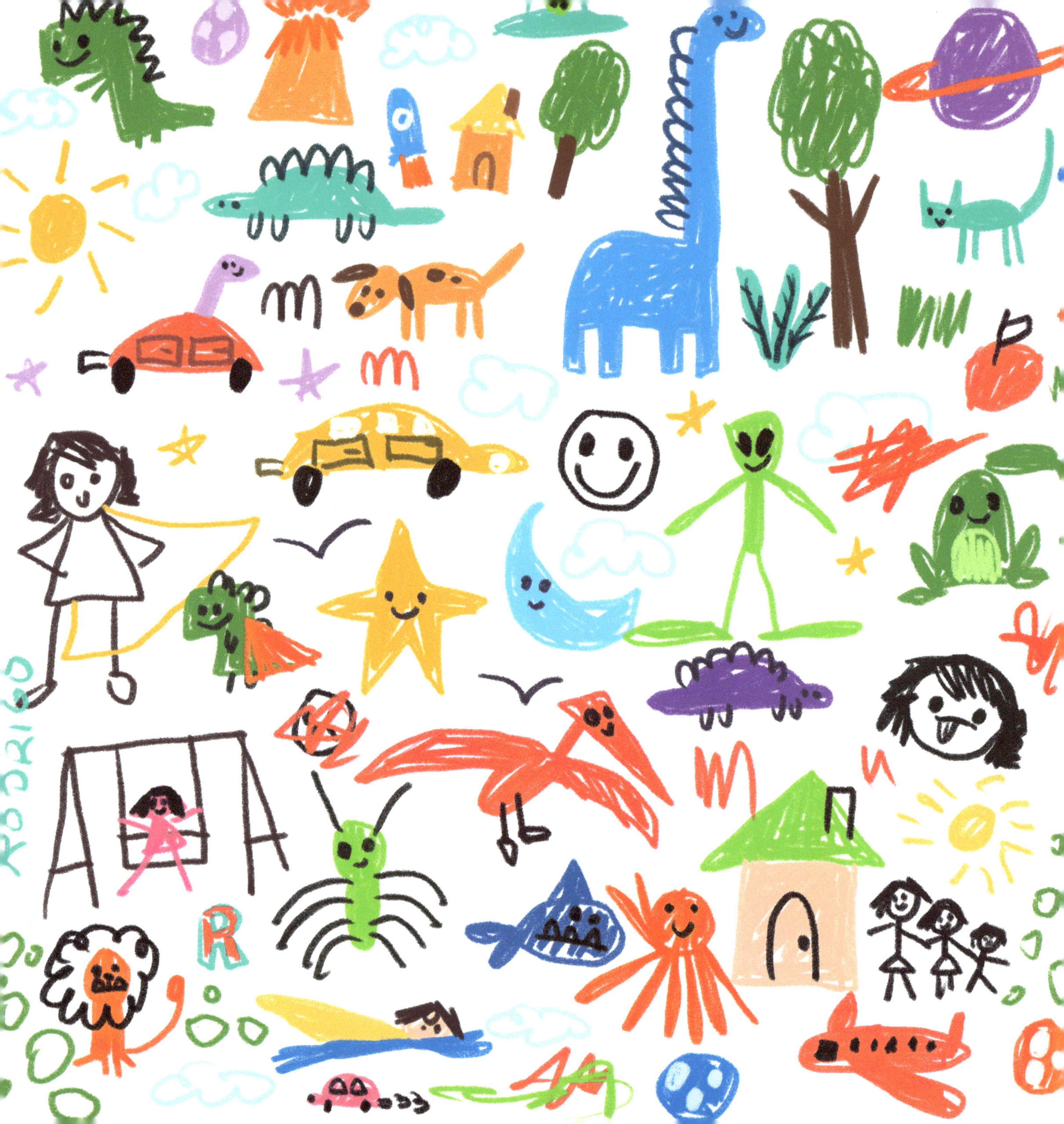
RODRIGO

CPSIA information can be obtained
at www.ICGtesting.com
Printed in the USA
BVHW012236220223
659058BV00001B/3

THE Royal FAMILY

Helen Cox Cannons

Raintree is an imprint of Capstone Global Library Limited, a company incorporated in England and Wales having its registered office at 264 Banbury Road, Oxford, OX2 7DY – Registered company number: 6695582

www.raintree.co.uk
myorders@raintree.co.uk

Text © Capstone Global Library Limited 2019
The moral rights of the proprietor have been asserted

All rights reserved. No part of this publication may be reproduced in any form or by any means (including photocopying or storing it in any medium by electronic means and whether or not transiently or incidentally to some other use of this publication) without the written permission of the copyright owner, except in accordance with the provisions of the Copyright, Designs and Patents Act 1988 or under the terms of a licence issued by the Copyright Licensing Agency, Saffron House, 6–10 Kirby Street, London EC1N 8TS (www.cla.co.uk). Applications for the copyright owner's written permission should be addressed to the publisher.

Edited by Clare Lewis
Designed by Dynamo Limited
Original illustrations © Capstone Global Library Limited 2019
Picture research by Dynamo Limited
Production by Helen McCreath
Originated by Capstone Global Library Limited
Printed and bound in India

ISBN 978 1 4747 7293 8 (hardback)
23 22 21 20 19
10 9 8 7 6 5 4 3 2 1

ISBN 978 1 4747 7295 2 (paperback)
24 23 22 21 20
10 9 8 7 6 5 4 3 2 1

British Library Cataloguing in Publication Data
A full catalogue record for this book is available from the British Library.

Acknowledgements
We would like to thank the following for permission to reproduce photographs: Alamy: Jonathan Clarke, 29, Michael Dunlea, 6, Julie Edwards, Cover, 28, 29, Trevor Holt, 23, 29, Newscom, 7, PA Images/Kirsty Wigglesworth, 4, Xinhua/Stephen Chung, 20, 28; Getty Images: 500Px Plus/Catalina Panait, 25 Center Right, AFP/ Aaron Chown, 19, 28, AFP/Heathcliff O'Malley, 16, 28, David M. Benett, 29, DigitalVision Vectors/ duncan1890, 5, Gamma-Rapho/Keystone-France, 10, Tim Graham, 12, 13, 28, Hulton Archive/Central Press/Leonard Burt, 15, Hulton Archive/Fox Photos, 27, Hulton Archive/PNA, 8, Anwar Hussein Collection/MoD/Ian Holding, 18, Indigo/Max Mumby, 22, 29, iStock/argalis, 25 Bottom Left, iStock Editorial/IR_Stone, 25 Top Left, iStock Editorial/johnkellerman, 24 Left, iStock Editorial/Pat_Hastings, 24 Right, David Jones- WPA Pool, 17, 28, Dominic Lipinski/WPA Pool, 28, Eamonn McCormack, 11, 28, Rolls Press/Popperfoto, 26, UKPress/Mark Cuthbert, 28, UK Press/Antony Jones/Julian Parker, 14, 28, 29, Stuart C. Wilson, 29, WireImage/Samir Hussein 21, 28; Superstock/akg-images, 9.

Every effort has been made to contact copyright holders of material reproduced in this book. Any omissions will be rectified in subsequent printings if notice is given to the publisher.

All the internet addresses (URLs) given in this book were valid at the time of going to press. However, due to the dynamic nature of the internet, some addresses may have changed, or sites may have changed or ceased to exist since publication. While the author and publisher regret any inconvenience this may cause readers, no responsibility for any such changes can be accepted by either the author or the publisher.

Contents

Meet the British royal family 4
What does the royal family do? 6
The Queen 8
Prince Philip 10
Prince Charles 12
Princess Anne, Prince Andrew and Prince Edward 14
Prince William 16
Prince Harry 18
Prince George, Princess Charlotte and Prince Louis 20
Other members of the royal family 22
Royal palaces and houses 24
Royal pets 26
The royal family tree 28
Glossary 30
Find out more 31
Index 32

Some words are shown in bold, **like this**. You can find out what they mean by looking in the glossary.

Meet the British royal family

The British royal family is known all over the world. The head of the royal family is our queen, Queen Elizabeth II. She is also Head of the **Commonwealth** of Nations. Elizabeth II is the queen of 16 countries within the Commonwealth, including Australia, Canada, Jamaica, New Zealand, Papua New Guinea and the Solomon Islands. Her family helps to support her in her role.

The Queen and the royal family are popular all over the world.

King Athelstan ruled for 15 years.

ATHELSTAN.

There have been kings and queens in England and Britain for over 1,500 years. Before that, there were kings and queens of different tribes or groups of people. It is believed that the first king of all of England was Athelstan. He **reigned** from AD 924 to AD 939.

What does the royal family do?

Members of the royal family carry out over 2,000 official **engagements** each year. They host events at palaces, present people with awards and open new buildings. They also support around 3,000 charities and public organizations. Many royals, including Prince Charles, Prince William and Prince Harry, have served in the **armed forces**.

Prince Charles is a general in the Army, admiral in the Navy and Air Chief Marshall in the RAF.

The royals often travel to different countries. They **represent** Britain and meet important leaders. The Queen has travelled to over 120 countries in her lifetime. When the royals travel, lots of people come and wave flags to welcome them. The Queen wears bright colours so she can be seen in a crowd.

Royal Fact!
Members of the royal family receive around 100,000 letters a year. Their staff helps them with all those replies!

Prince William visited Japan in 2015.

The Queen

Princess Elizabeth and her little sister, Princess Margaret, played together as children.

Queen Elizabeth II was born on 21 April 1926. Her father was King George VI (1895–1952) and her mother was Queen Elizabeth (later known as the Queen Mother). As a young princess, Elizabeth had a happy childhood with her sister, Princess Margaret. In 1947, at the age of 21, she married Prince Philip. They have four children: Prince Charles, Princess Anne, Prince Andrew and Prince Edward.

On 6 February 1952, King George VI died. Elizabeth became Queen Elizabeth II. Her **coronation** took place on 2 June 1953 in Westminster Abbey.

The Queen is also Supreme Governor of the Church of England. This means she appoints leaders within the Church of England. Now in her nineties, the Queen is Britain's longest-**reigning** monarch. She celebrated 65 years on the throne in February 2017.

Before the Queen's coronation, many people did not own a television. A lot of people bought their first set specially for the event!

Prince Philip

The Queen and Prince Philip on the Buckingham Palace balcony in 1953

Prince Philip is the Queen's husband. He was born Philip, Prince of Greece and Denmark, in 1921. He grew up in Britain and went to Royal Naval College. Philip served in the Royal Navy during World War II (1939–45). In 1947 he became a British **citizen**. This meant he lost his right to the Greek and Danish thrones.

Prince Philip married Princess Elizabeth in Westminster Abbey on 20 November 1947. On their wedding day, Philip was given the title Duke of Edinburgh. Their wedding was heard on the radio by over 200 million people around the world. Philip has worked hard as the Queen's **Consort** over the years. In 2017, aged 96, he **retired** from royal duties.

Royal Fact!

Prince Philip is known for his naughty sense of humour. When his first son, Prince Charles, was born, Philip said, "He looks like a plum pudding!"

The Queen and Prince Philip have been married for more than 70 years.

Prince Charles

Charles and Diana's marriage did not last. They were **divorced** in 1996.

Prince Charles was born on 14 November 1948. He is the oldest son of the Queen and Prince Philip. Charles became Prince of Wales in 1969. At that time, he was studying at Cambridge University. Charles trained in both the Royal Air Force and the Royal Navy. In 1981, Charles married Lady Diana Spencer. Charles and Diana had two sons, Prince William and Prince Henry (known as Harry).

Diana died in a car accident in 1997. It was a difficult time for Charles and the two young princes. In 2005, Charles married Camilla, Duchess of Cornwall. They live at Clarence House in London. Charles is **heir** to the throne. He could become king at an unusually old age. He is already in his seventies.

Royal Fact!
Charles wrote a children's book in 1980. It was called *The Old Man of Lochnagar.* Charles made up the story when he was young to amuse his younger brothers, Andrew and Edward.

Prince Charles and Camilla, Duchess of Cornwall, on their wedding day

Princess Anne, Prince Andrew and Prince Edward

Prince Andrew (left), Prince Edward (middle) and Princess Anne

The Queen and Prince Philip had three other children after Prince Charles. Princess Anne was born in 1950 and is known as the Princess Royal. Prince Andrew was born in 1960 and is known as the Duke of York. Prince Edward was born in 1964 and is known as the Earl of Wessex. Anne, Andrew and Edward have two children each.

Diana died in a car accident in 1997. It was a difficult time for Charles and the two young princes. In 2005, Charles married Camilla, Duchess of Cornwall. They live at Clarence House in London. Charles is **heir** to the throne. He could become king at an unusually old age. He is already in his seventies.

Royal Fact!
Charles wrote a children's book in 1980. It was called *The Old Man of Lochnagar*. Charles made up the story when he was young to amuse his younger brothers, Andrew and Edward.

Prince Charles and Camilla, Duchess of Cornwall, on their wedding day

Princess Anne, Prince Andrew and Prince Edward

Prince Andrew (left), Prince Edward (middle) and Princess Anne

The Queen and Prince Philip had three other children after Prince Charles. Princess Anne was born in 1950 and is known as the Princess Royal. Prince Andrew was born in 1960 and is known as the Duke of York. Prince Edward was born in 1964 and is known as the Earl of Wessex. Anne, Andrew and Edward have two children each.

Charles, Anne, Andrew and Edward support many charities. They go on many **state visits** abroad that the Queen is now too old to make herself. In 2017, Anne, Andrew and Edward performed 1,166 **engagements** between them! These included 12 state visits by Prince Andrew, who travels abroad the most.

Royal Fact!
Princess Anne is an excellent horserider. She was the first ever British royal to compete at an Olympic Games – in Montreal, Canada in 1976.

Princess Anne is now President of the British Olympic Association.

Prince William

Prince William is the oldest son of Prince Charles and Princess Diana. He was born on 21 June 1982. After Prince Charles, William is next in line to the throne. He is close to his brother, Harry, and they still live in nearby apartments at Kensington Palace. William has served in the British Army, Royal Navy and Royal Air Force.

Prince William worked as an air ambulance pilot from 2015 to 2017.

William and Catherine married on a Friday. The day was made a public holiday so that people did not have to work.

On 29 April 2011, Prince William married Catherine (Kate) Middleton. On their wedding day, the couple became the Duke and Duchess of Cambridge. The wedding took place in Westminster Abbey. It was watched by 1,900 guests in the church – and millions outside it! William and Catherine now have three children: Prince George, Princess Charlotte and Prince Louis.

Prince Harry

Prince Harry (whose birth name is Henry) is Prince William's younger brother. He was born on 15 September 1984. Harry was in the British Army. He left the Army in 2015. In 2014, Harry set up the Invictus Games. This is a yearly sports competition for people injured, wounded or sick from their work in the **armed forces**.

Prince Harry fought in the war in Afghanistan.

Prince Harry and Meghan were married at Windsor Castle.

On 19 May 2018, Harry married Meghan Markle, an American actress. On their wedding day, they became the Duke and Duchess of Sussex. Harry and Meghan plan to do lots of charity work together. For their wedding, they asked guests to give money to charity instead of buying them gifts.

Royal Fact!

Harry is a big sports fan. He supports Arsenal football club and the England rugby team.

Prince George, Princess Charlotte and Prince Louis

William and Catherine's oldest child, Prince George, was born on 22 July 2013. He is in line to **inherit** the throne one day, after William. When George was born, **21-gun salutes** announced his birth. George started at primary school in September 2017.

Royal Fact!
George is a trend-setter for the clothes he wears. He was named in Tatler magazine's "2018 Best Dressed" list!

Prince George and Princess Charlotte went to visit their new baby brother in hospital.

William and Catherine showed baby Prince Louis to the world outside the hospital where he was born.

Princess Charlotte was born on 2 May 2015. When she was born, famous London places such as Tower Bridge, the London Eye and the Trafalgar Square fountains were lit up in pink. Charlotte started at nursery school near her home in Kensington Palace in January 2018. Prince Louis was born on 23 April 2018. On the evening of his birth, famous London places were lit up in blue.

Other members of the royal family

Princess Eugenie (left) and Princess Beatrice

The Queen has eight grandchildren. She also has seven great-grandchildren. When a royal baby is born, the Queen must be the first person to know about it.

Princess Beatrice and Princess Eugenie are granddaughters of the Queen. Their parents are Prince Andrew and Sarah, Duchess of York.

The Queen's granddaughter Zara Tindall is a keen horserider like her mother, Princess Anne. She took part in the Olympics in 2012. She won a team silver medal. Zara is married to Mike Tindall, who played rugby for England. They have two daughters, Mia and Lena.

Royal Fact!
Some of the Queen's great-grandchildren call her "Gan-Gan".

Zara Tindall riding in a competition

Royal palaces and houses

There are many royal palaces and houses around Britain. The Queen and Prince Philip spend time in them throughout the year. Some palaces are **permanent** homes to other members of the royal family.

Buckingham Palace
Buckingham Palace is the official London home of the Queen. It is where she does her work and hosts many events. It has a huge balcony that the royal family often stand on for special events.

Kensington Palace
Kensington Palace is also in London. Today, it is the home and workplace of Prince William and the Duchess of Cambridge, and Prince Harry and the Duchess of Sussex.

Windsor Castle

Windsor Castle is the largest lived-in castle in the world. The Queen often spends her weekends at Windsor Castle. She also lives there for a month at Easter time.

The Palace of Holyroodhouse

The Palace of Holyroodhouse in Edinburgh is the official palace of the Queen in Scotland. The Queen spends one week there every year, known as "Holyrood Week".

Balmoral Castle

Balmoral Castle is a royal holiday home. The Queen and other members of the royal family go to Balmoral for their summer holidays.

Royal pets

Just like in many families, pets have always been important to the royal family. The King Charles spaniel is named after King Charles II, who was king from 1660 to 1685. As well as dogs, many royal kings and queens have kept horses. The Queen is an excellent horserider. One of her horses, named Burmese, was a gift from the **Royal Canadian Mounted Police.**

The Queen rode Burmese at the **Trooping the Colour** ceremony for 18 years in a row.

Royal Fact!

The Queen's dogs Willow, Monty and Holly acted with the Queen in a short film for the 2012 London Olympics. They met Daniel Craig, who was dressed as his film character James Bond, when he came to meet the Queen at Buckingham Palace!

The Queen's dogs are often photographed with her.

The Queen is known for owning corgis, which are a breed of dog. She has owned more than 30 during her **reign** but her last corgi, Willow, died in 2018. She now has two "dorgis", Candy and Vulcan. She invented the dorgi cross-breed when her sister Princess Margaret's dachshund Pipkin **mated** with one of the Queen's corgis.

The royal family tree

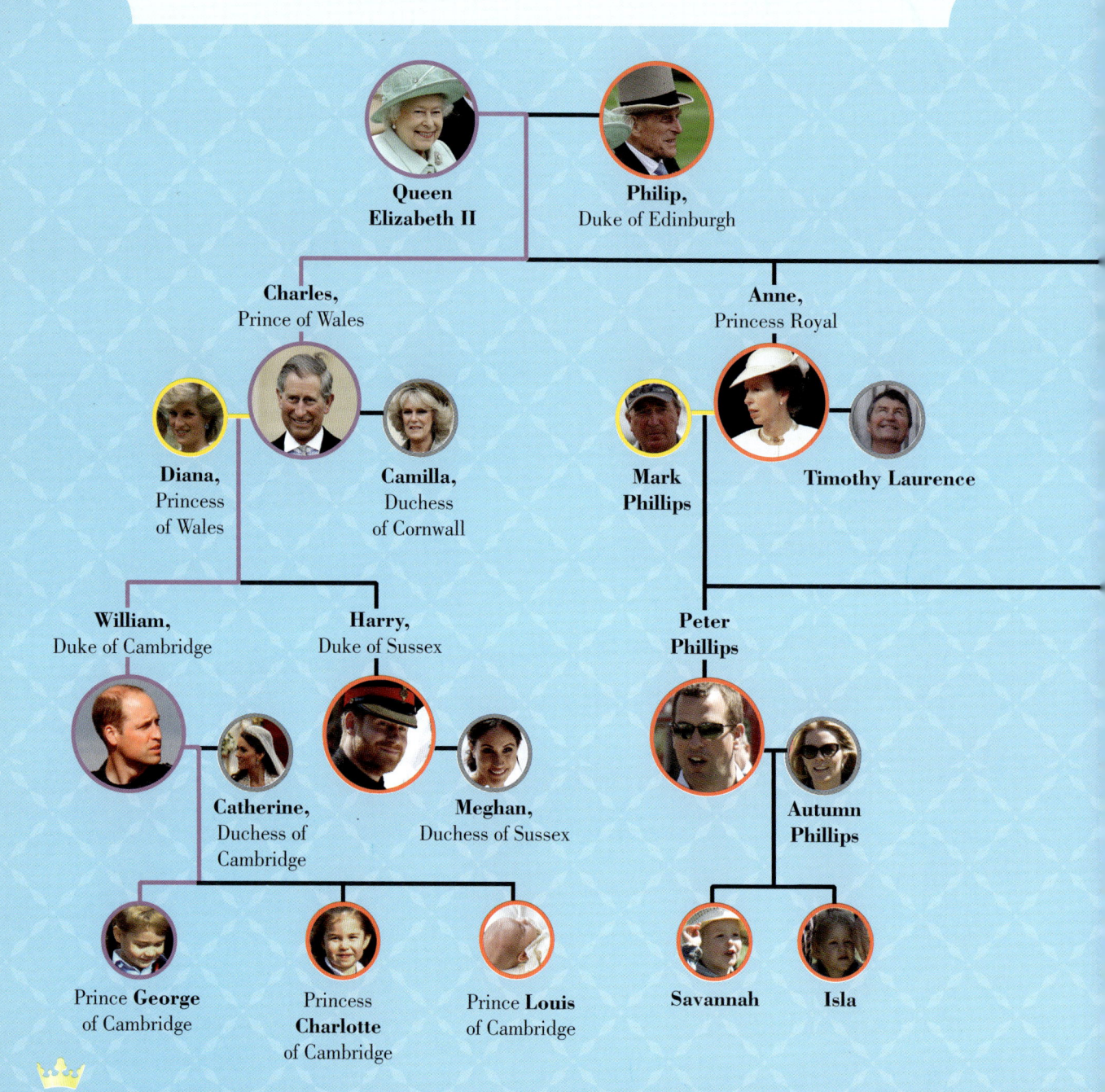

Queen Elizabeth II — **Philip,** Duke of Edinburgh

Charles, Prince of Wales
- **Diana,** Princess of Wales
- **Camilla,** Duchess of Cornwall

Anne, Princess Royal
- **Mark Phillips**
- **Timothy Laurence**

William, Duke of Cambridge — **Catherine,** Duchess of Cambridge

Harry, Duke of Sussex — **Meghan,** Duchess of Sussex

Peter Phillips — **Autumn Phillips**

Prince **George** of Cambridge

Princess **Charlotte** of Cambridge

Prince **Louis** of Cambridge

Savannah

Isla

28

It is most likely that Prince Charles will become the next monarch if the Queen retires, **abdicates** or dies. He is the **heir** to the throne. There is a list of royals who could **inherit** the throne. We call it "the line of succession". Each time a royal baby is born, the line of succession can change. This is a royal family tree, showing the line of succession.

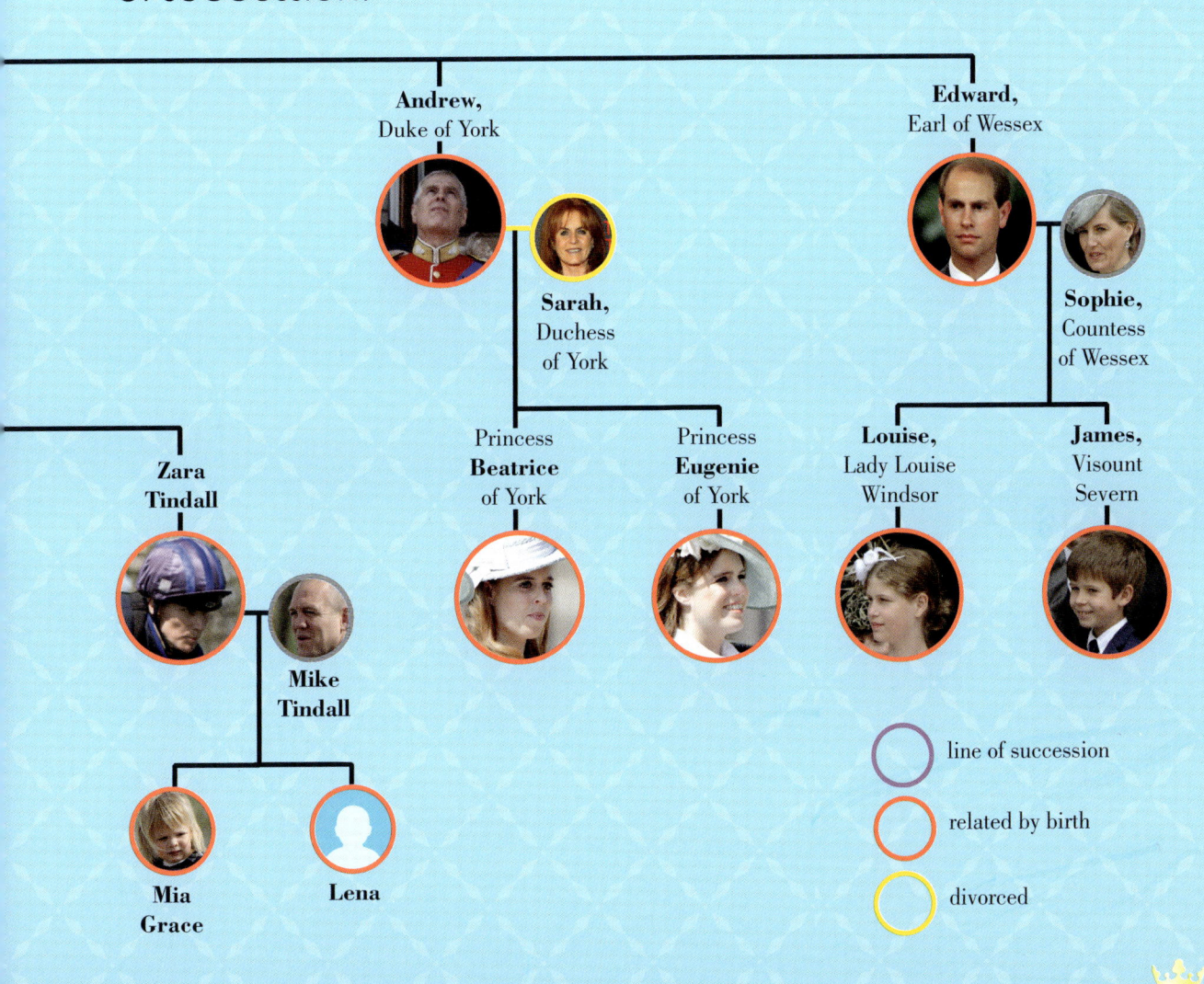

Andrew, Duke of York

Sarah, Duchess of York

Edward, Earl of Wessex

Sophie, Countess of Wessex

Zara Tindall

Mike Tindall

Princess **Beatrice** of York

Princess **Eugenie** of York

Louise, Lady Louise Windsor

James, Visount Severn

Mia Grace

Lena

○ line of succession
○ related by birth
○ divorced

29

Glossary

21-gun salute when 21 shots are fired out of cannons by soldiers to celebrate a special royal event

abdicate choose to stop being the king or queen

armed forces there are three branches of the armed forces: the British Army, the Royal Navy and the Royal Air Force

citizen legal member of a country

Commonwealth group of countries around the world made up of the UK and states that used to be part of the British Empire

consort person a king or queen is married to

coronation ceremony of the official crowning of a king or queen

divorce official ending to a marriage

engagement arrangement to go somewhere or do something at a fixed time

heir person who inherits the title and work of the person before them

inherit receive from someone when that person dies

mate when a male and female animal join together to produce young

permanent all the time

reign rule as king or queen

represent act on behalf of everyone

Royal Canadian Mounted Police national police force of Canada, created in 1873. They are known around the world as "the Mounties" because they ride on horseback.

state visit ceremonial visit to another country by the Queen or another member of the royal family

Trooping the Colour official birthday parade to celebrate the Queen's birthday. It involves soldiers, horses and musicians marching from Buckingham Palace, down the Mall, to Horse Guard's Parade. Members of the royal family take part as well, in carriages or on horseback.

Find out more

Books
Queen Elizabeth II, Vic Parker (Raintree, 2012)
Queen Elizabeth II: Her Story, John Malam (Wayland, 2016)
Queen Elizabeth II (Info Buzz: History), Izzi Howell (Franklin Watts, 2018)

Website
www.royal.uk
Everything you need to know about members of the royal family is here on their official website.

Places to visit
Many royal palaces and homes are open to visitors. Here is a list of some of the most popular royal places to visit. Each website has information on visiting times.

Balmoral Castle & Estate, Ballater AB35 5TB
www.royal.uk/royal-residences-balmoral-castle

Buckingham Palace, Westminster, London SW1A 1AA
www.royalcollection.org.uk/visit/the-state-rooms-buckingham-palace

Edinburgh Castle, Castlehill, Edinburgh EH1 2NG
www.edinburghcastle.scot

Hampton Court Palace, Molesey, East Molesey KT8 9AU
www.hrp.org.uk/hampton-court-palace/#gs.ugYIw=c

Kensington Palace, Kensington Gardens, London W8 4PX
www.hrp.org.uk/kensington-palace/#gs.i8qISMA

Palace of Holyroodhouse, Canongate, Edinburgh EH8 8DX
www.royalcollection.org.uk/visit/palace-of-holyroodhouse

Tower of London, St Katharine's & Wapping, London EC3N 4AB
www.hrp.org.uk/tower-of-london/#gs.yEOvrHO

Windsor Castle, Windsor SL4 1NJ
www.royalcollection.org.uk/visit/windsorcastle

Index

armed forces 6, 10, 16, 18
Camilla, Duchess of Cornwall 13
Catherine, Duchess of
Cambridge 17, 20, 21
Church of England 9
Commonwealth 4
coronation 9
dogs 27
Diana, Princess of Wales 12, 13
family tree 28–29
horses 15, 26
Invictus Games 18
King Athelstan 5
King George VI 8, 9
Meghan Markle 19
Mike Tindall 23
Olympic Games 15, 23, 27
palaces and houses 24–25
pets 26–27

Prince Andrew 8, 13, 14–15, 22
Prince Charles 6, 8, 11, 12–13
Prince Edward 8, 13, 14–15
Prince George 17, 20
Prince Harry 6, 12, 18–19
Prince Louis 17, 21
Prince Philip 8, 9–10, 14
Prince William 6, 12, 16–17, 18, 20, 21
Princess Anne 8, 14–15, 23
Princess Beatrice 22
Princess Charlotte 17, 21
Princess Eugenie 22
Princess Margaret 8
Queen Elizabeth II 4, 7, 8–9, 10, 11, 14, 22, 23
Queen Mother 8
Sarah, Duchess of York 22
succession 28–29
travel 7, 15
Trooping the Colour 26
weddings 11, 12, 13, 17, 19
Zara Tindall 23